Ms. Wen

H getting to know you, & I look fwd to continuing the connection! May you feel God as you read through each page ♡

HEALING
Revelations

Brittney J. Lyons

HEALING Revelations
See Life In It All

BRITTNEY J. LYONS

HEALING REVELATIONS
See Life In It All

Copyright © 2019 by Brittney J. Lyons
All rights reserved.

All rights reserved. This book is protected by the copyright laws of the United States of America. This book may not be copied or reprinted for commercial gain or profit. The use of quotations or occasional page copying for personal or group study is permitted and encouraged. Permission will be granted upon request.

Unless otherwise identified, Scripture quotations are from the King James Version. Copyright © 1982 by Thomas Nelson, Inc. Used by permission. All rights reserved.

Scripture quotations marked "NKJV" are taken from the New King James Version. Copyright © 1982 by Thomas Nelson, Inc. Used by permission. All rights reserved.

Scripture quotations marked (NLT) are taken from the Holy Bible, New Living Translation, copyright © 1996. Used by permission of Tyndale House Publishers, Inc., Wheaton, IL 60189 USA. All rights reserved.

Final Step Publishing, LLC

PO Box 1441
Suffolk, VA 23439

For Worldwide Distribution. Printed in U.S.A.

Soft cover ISBN: 978-0-578-13221-1
E-Book ISBN: 978-1-733-58420-3

Library of Congress: 2019931275

Cover & Interior Design: Cooke Consulting & Creations

CONTENTS

Acknowledgements	9
Introduction	11
Healing Revelation 1: I Am Healed	13
Healing Revelation 2: I Am Forgiven	17
Healing Revelation 3: I Speak Life Over Every Dead Place	21
Healing Revelation 4: I Am Free	25
Healing Revelation 5: I Don't Have to be Afraid Because I've Got God's Presence	29
Healing Revelation 6: I Can Handle Change	33
Healing Revelation 7: God is Perfecting My Faith	37
Healing Revelation 8: I Have a New Mind	41
Healing Revelation 9: I Am Pregnant with God's Promises	45
Healing Revelation 10: I Am Not Who I Used to Be	47

Healing Revelation 11:   51
I Have What It Takes to Win

Healing Revelation 12:   55
I Yield to God's Voice

Healing Revelation 13:   59
I Have a Purpose for Living

Healing Revelation 14:   63
I Am Not Bound by the Wound pt. 1

Healing Revelation 15:   67
I Am Not Bound by the Wound pt. 2

Healing Revelation 16:   71
I Am Not Bound by the Wound pt. 3

Healing Revelation 17:   75
Reader's Choice

I dedicate this book to my God. Through every problem I've faced, You have truly helped me to see *life in it all.*

Acknowledgements

First and foremost, to my Creator, Healer, Keeper, Protector, Provider, Friend, and my all in all, God the Father, Jesus Christ the Son, and the Holy Spirit, I thank You for giving me life and for birthing life out of me and into this book. Lord Jesus, You are awesome! Thank You for counting me worthy enough to die on the cross for me. I thank You for shedding Your blood so that healing could manifest in my life, and because You live, I live. Holy Spirit, thank You for never leaving me alone but for comforting me in my low places, filling me with joy, and surrounding me with peace. Thank You for leading, teaching, and guiding me into God's perfect will for my life.

To my amazing husband, Joseph, thank you for pushing and encouraging me to be the woman, wife, and writer that God has created me to be. I thank God for allowing my life to be blessed with your presence, partnership, prayers, and love. I love you so much, and I look forward to what God has in store for us NEXT!

To my wonderful parents, Donnie Jones, Caroltine S. Bowles, and Larry Bowles, thank you for introducing me to Christ at an early age. Thank you for raising me up to know God, love God, and serve God. I also thank you for allowing me to be exactly who God predetermined that I would be. I love you all.

To my parents-in-love, Mr. Joseph and Pastor Tracey Lyons, thank you two for always supporting me, encouraging me, and believing in the gifts God put in me.

A big thank you to Final Step Publishing for pushing forward the vision that God planted in me. Your leadership, guidance, and professionalism is genuine and greatly appreciated!

I personally would like to thank my mentor, Dr. Antipas Harris. God used you to plant a seed in the author in me. May God bless you and your family.

I must thank my pastor, Pastor Alvin Georges. Thank you for your leadership and prayers. I also thank you for allowing me the opportunity to be who God called me to be.

Last but certainly not least, I want to say thank you to Pastor Kim White, Dr. Angel White, Dr. Dwight and Dr. Jennell Riddick, Min. Sherenda Jones, and Min. Nija Means for helping me to recognize, carry, and give birth to the healing ministry in my life. God has used each of you for a specific purpose along this journey.

Introduction

In the book of Romans, the Bible declares that everything we go through in life, be it good, bad, ugly, or undecided, must work out for our good, i.e., in our favor (Romans 8:28). There is absolutely nothing that you are facing right now, have faced in the past, or will face in the future, that will not yield you a good result. There is a blessing in the midst of pain, heartache, and brokenness. Healing is not just for the one who scraped their knee, but there is healing for those who may have received an unfavorable report from the doctor, those who think their life is a mistake, and even for those who may be stuck in a dead situation. The hardest thing to do is seeing that healing while in the middle of the struggle. Visualize, for a moment, yourself walking or driving through an actual storm. It's cloudy, windy, and rain is pouring down. Is your vision clear? Probably not. During a storm, it's harder to see clearly with our physical eyes. However, we are challenged to walk by our faith (spiritual eyes) and not by what we see physically (2 Corinthians 5:7). This book was designed to do just that—help you see the blessing in the midst of the struggle and to see healing in place of pain.

In this book you will find 16 Healing Revelations to read through and declare over your life. These revelations are not just titles, but they are declarations that I encourage you to speak over your life each day. If you divide the number sixteen in half, you have eight, and this is the number of new beginnings. Birthing this book was a new beginning for me, however, I am believing by faith that as you read through this book, a new beginning will be birthed for you too (8x2=a new beginning for me and one for you). My prayer is that a new beginning will be manifested in the form of healing in your relationships, marriage, family, business/ministry, emotions, mind, and body. Please know that I have prayed for you before this book was placed into your hands.

Yes, hard times are difficult to embrace, but with the Holy Spirit's guidance, it is my prayer that as you read through each Healing Revelation, you will begin to truly *see life in it all*.

Healing Revelation 1:
I Am Healed
John 5:1-9

In John chapter 5, there is the introduction of a man who had been lying by a pool called Bethesda. This man had been dealing with a sickness for a very long time—thirty-eight years. For thirty-eight years, all he knew was his condition. The Bible states that he is a lame man. According to the dictionary, when one is lame, it means to be "crippled or physically disabled, especially in the foot or leg as to limp or walk with difficulty." Synonyms of the word lame are "inadequate," "ineffective," and "insufficient." The Bible doesn't even give this man a name; he is just called 'a lame man.' He is only identified by his condition. He's only recognized as being inadequate, ineffective, and insufficient. So, for thirty-eight years, he has been feeling like an outsider. Maybe he's felt as though his life and existence served no purpose.

Perhaps you know what it feels like to be identified by your condition, circumstance, or failures. Are you currently experiencing inadequacies in your life? Does it seem like there is one area where you feel ineffective? Or maybe because of what you are going through, the support you would like to have from others is insufficient. Have you gone through your entire life feeling like an outsider? Or maybe because you have experienced more hardship than happiness, you are led to believe that your existence serves no purpose.

If you can answer 'yes' to any of these questions, then I must tell you that there is good news for you! The lame man in the text met his good news in verse 6. John 5:6 reads, "When Jesus saw him and knew he had been ill for a long time, he asked him, 'Would you like to get well?'" (NLT) In spite of what this man had faced for so long and regardless that others saw him as an outsider,

Jesus offered him a solution that no one else could have offered—He offered him *healing*.

This kind of healing was not just physical. But I believe that Jesus offered him an emotional, mental, and spiritual healing as well. This man waited thirty-eight years to be healed from his condition. I can only imagine that year after year seeing that his healing was not in his reach, perhaps he began to lose hope that he *could* be healed. That is why once Jesus asked him if he wanted to be healed the man gives Jesus reasons why he hasn't been healed (John 5:7). I believe that Jesus could sense the hopelessness and despair in this man's response; therefore, instead of asking him anymore questions, Jesus gives the man a command in verse 8 that is an extension of the healing that Jesus offered in verse 6. "Jesus told him, 'Stand up, pick up your mat, and walk!'" (NLT) After this command, the Bible tells us that the man was instantly healed, got up, and began to walk! He now had the ability to do something that he probably could not do in the last thirty-eight years of his life! It is important to note that nowhere in the text do we see Jesus helping the man get up to walk. Jesus simply spoke a Word to the man that would bring forth his healing; however, the man also had to do something—he had to believe in the Word that he received from Jesus. He had to believe Jesus for something that he had never done. He had to believe Jesus for a healing that he had not known. His believing the Word had to be shown in his actions. He got up, picked up his mat, and began to walk! He literally walked out the healing that Jesus gave.

My friend, what is *your* condition? Have you received an unfavorable report from the doctor (physical)? Have you had to walk away from certain relationships (emotional)? Do you have a fear of what the future holds (mental)? Or are you disinterested in joining a new church because of past church hurt (spiritual)? What kind of healing do you need from God? All healing comes from God, but the first step to receiving healing starts in *your* mind. Do you even believe that you can be healed? Let me encourage you, YES, YOU CAN! If God can heal a man who had been ill for thirty-eight years, surely He can and will do more for you! Forget what the devil told you, God is a HEALER and He wants to HEAL YOU! Believe God to do something that you have not been able to do before. Believe God to open your new business, start your own ministry, write your first book, have a healthy marriage, and even heal your broken heart. Believe God for your healing! If you have been stuck in a condition, be it physical, mental, emotional or even spiritual, your good news is this: this is the day that Jesus sees you, and He is asking, "Would *you* like to get well?" Now what will be **your** response? I encourage you to open your mouth and say these three powerful words with me, "I am healed!"

So, together, let us lay our conditions on the altar and believe God for healing. I encourage you to write down your conditions on the line(s) below, and watch God heal:

The condition may be _____
But I Am Healed!

The condition may be _____
But I Am Healed!

The condition may be _____
But I Am Healed!

The condition may be _____
But I Am Healed!

The condition may be _____
But I Am Healed!

Your healing revelation for today and every day is to open your mouth and declare that YOU ARE HEALED! No matter how big or small the condition, YOU ARE HEALED!

Now, say it with me: I Am Healed In Jesus' Name!

P.S. The more you say it, the more you will believe it!

Healing Revelation 2:
I Am Forgiven
1 John 1:9

Say it with me: I am not perfect, but I am forgiven. Now say it with some meaning: I Am Not Perfect, BUT I AM FORGIVEN!

The enemy wants you to believe that if you mess up, that's it— i.e., God doesn't love you anymore and life is no longer worth living. Jesus warns us of the devil's primary goal which is "to steal and kill and destroy" (John 10:10 NLT). The enemy waits for you to slip up. He's been waiting for you to curse them out, get drunk, tell that lie, gossip, or to miss a few Sundays of worship which, eventually, turn into years of isolation from the church. The moment you mess up, the enemy's plan is to make you feel like you are the worst person that was ever created. He's been plotting to steal your joy of living a happy life. He's already planned to kill every dream that you are chasing, and he's already set up the day and hour when he wants to destroy your hope in God. Does this sound familiar? The Bible teaches to not be surprised when these kinds of attacks come your way as if something strange and weird were just happening to you (1 Peter 4:12). The devil is after your relationship with God, and he will do everything in his power to make you believe that because you have sinned, God no longer wants to deal with you. But I'd like to offer a different thought. *When,* not *if,* you mess up, it's OK; it's not the end of the world, and God still loves you!

I am believing that today is the last day that you feel any guilt or shame because of your hiccups in life. First John 1:9 says this, "But if we confess our sins to him, he is faithful and just to forgive us our sins and to cleanse us from all wickedness" (NLT). So what, you messed up! If you simply confess your sins to God,

He will forgive you. God loves you, and He does not want you to carry the burden of feeling shameful. That is a trick of the enemy! I know because he's done the same thing to me. I used to be so down on myself for messing up that I began to lose focus of the assignments that God placed in my life. Once I realized that God was no longer holding my sins against me and once I confessed them to Him, I had to stop holding myself hostage. Friend, free yourself from your mistakes. Confess your sins to God and then let them go. Don't allow the devil to lie to you and make you feel as though you will never recover from what you did.

The devil is not stronger than God, and God does not make us feel worth-less, but His Word reminds us that because He gave us His son Jesus (John 3:16), He thinks we are worth it. Now, my friend, it is time for you to live in freedom because YOU ARE FORGIVEN!

By completing this exercise, you are making a step towards living a guilt-free life. Pray with me:

Most Holy God,

Thank You for seeing me as somebody that is worth loving. Your Word declares that if I confess my sins to You, You will not only forgive me, but will cleanse me from the things that do not bring You glory. So, God, right now, I confess my sins to You, and I thank You that because of this moment, I am Forgiven.

In Jesus' name, Amen.

I Am Forgiven from _____
_____

I Am Forgiven from _____
_____

I Am Forgiven from _____

_____

I Am Forgiven from _____

_____

I Am Forgiven from _____

_____

*You are encouraged to continue creating a list of the things you are forgiven from on another source, like a journal, notebook, tablet, etc.

Healing Revelation 3:
I Speak Life Over Every Dead Place
Acts 9:36-42

This story in Acts 9 highlights a disciple of Christ named Tabitha (Greek name is Dorcas). She was noted to have done many wonderful deeds as she "was always doing kind things for others and helping the poor" (Acts 9:36 NLT). Tabitha was the kind of woman that you wanted to have in your corner for you could most likely count on her to be there. Well, the time came and she became ill and died. As you would imagine, this brought grief and great sorrow to the people of her community. At the time she died, some believers in her community heard that Peter, the man of God, was nearby, so they sent for him to come. Peter came, and when he arrived, they took him straight to Tabitha's body. When Peter got to the room where the body of Tabitha was lying, there were widows in the room weeping over her death. Peter asked them to leave the room, and once they left, he prayed. After praying, Peter turned to the body and said, "Get up, Tabitha," (Acts 9:40 NLT) and indeed, she got up!

Peter teaches us a critical lesson in this story: just because something has died doesn't mean it can't come back to life. Peter believed God to bring something back to life that had died. Peter chose to believe for LIFE in place of death.

Has something died in your life? Gifts? Dreams? Ministry? Marriage? Business? If you can identify that something has in fact died, do you believe that God has the power to bring it back to life? Now, let's be clear, there are some things in our lives that may have died because they needed to die. However, what things have died that God declared you shall have? What about your peace? Love? Joy? Hope? Has your happiness died? If anything has died in your life that God said you shall have, if you will believe, IT SHALL COME BACK TO LIFE AGAIN!

How you may be wondering. Well, let's look at what Peter did. He did three things that we can use in our own situations. First, he **established the right focus**. Peter asked all the widows who were weeping and crying to leave the room. All they could see was a dead situation, but Peter saw the possibility of LIFE. He established the right focus for creating an atmosphere where life could take place by removing everything that would remind him of what had died. In other words, he removed distractions. In order to believe God for something in your life to live, you must remove all distractions and establish the right focus to set the atmosphere for miracles to transpire in your life.

> Peter teaches us a critical lesson in this story: just because something has died doesn't mean it can't come back to life.

Who and what would only remind you of how bad things really are? If you are believing God for better health, then you may have to remove the people in your life that only remind you of how bad your condition is. If you are believing God for a financial breakthrough and relief, you may have to stop spending time with broke-minded people. You can't have anyone around you planning for a funeral when you are believing God for a resurrection! If you want to win, surround yourself with winners! If you want to survive, surround yourself with survivors!

Second, Peter **engaged with the Father**. After he asked the widows to leave the room, he then knelt and prayed. Peter knew that he could not handle the situation on his own. In fact, he knew that God was the only One with resurrecting power. He relied on the One that had the power to turn the situation around. YOU CAN NOT HANDLE THIS ON YOUR OWN! You need God to bring you through this. Daily, you must engage with God, whom is our Provider, our Keeper, our Help, our Protector, our Friend, and our Healer. Daily, you must desire to have His Presence manifested in your life. Besides, the only way that thing is going to LIVE is with God.

Third and finally, Peter **extended his faith**. After Peter prayed, he then spoke directly to the body of Tabitha and commanded her to get up! Indeed, she got up! I am challenging you to extend your faith to that kind of level. Begin to speak to the dead places (that are supposed to live) and command them to get up in Jesus' name! It takes faith to speak to something that is lifeless and believe it to have life. But, hey, without faith, we cannot please God (Hebrews 11:6). Will you take this challenge today? Don't just stop today, but let today be the start of a new beginning of your extended faith and begin to daily speak life over your mind, body, soul, and spirit. Speak life over your health, marriage, children, finances, ministry, and business.

Today your assignment is to simply create a list of the things that you desire to live in your life (according to the perfect Will of God for you). Then, by using your own mouth, declare into the atmosphere that it/they shall LIVE IN JESUS' NAME!

I Speak Life to _____

_____ and command it to get up in Jesus' name!

I Speak Life to _____

_____ and command it to get up in Jesus' name!

I Speak Life to _____

_____and command it to get up in Jesus' name!

I Speak Life to _____

_____ and command it to get up in Jesus' name!

Healing Revelation 4:
I Am Free
Luke 13:10-13; 16

Do you feel as though something in your life has control over you? Is it something bigger and stronger than you? Does it have a hold over you and prevent you from being totally free? Maybe you have a connection with someone who is not in the Will of God for you. Or maybe you are struggling with an addiction to something in your life. It's no fun being stuck in a situation that has taken away your freedom. Where there is an absence of freedom, there is also an absence of joy and peace. There are some struggles we face that are evil in nature, i.e., the cause of pain, misery, and torture, that are from an evil spirit which is Satan himself. It is the goal of the adversary to keep us confined and confused. To do this, he will use whatever he wants to try and accomplish this goal. In fact, there are some people that are on assignment from the enemy to plant seeds of distraction in your life. I encourage you to ask the Holy Spirit to reveal to you if there are people you are connected to that are only there to distract you from the things of God. Even if you find that you have been attacked by an evil spirit, God has the power to set you free.

Let's take a look at a woman who knows what it's like to be attacked by an evil spirit. Luke 13:10-16 highlights an interesting story of a woman who had been crippled by Satan. We learn that the attack caused her to be bent over for eighteen years. This means that for almost twenty years–two decades–she has not had the ability to freely move her body, especially her back, in any way she wanted. She was confined to one position that caused her to bend towards the ground whether she wanted to or not. This woman, as Jesus stated, was held in this position of bondage by Satan (verse 16). She was stuck in a situation that she couldn't get out of on her own.

Personally, I can identify with this woman. I have a brother who is ten years older than me. When I was around the age of eleven or twelve, which would have put him around the age of twenty-one or twenty-two, he loved to watch wrestling on TV. After watching a wrestling match and feeling empowered, he would then search for someone in the house on whom he could try out his new "moves." Well, since we didn't have any other siblings, I was usually the person of choice. My brother would put me in these wrestling holds that used to frustrate me! Now my brother is much bigger than I am and definitely much stronger physically. So when he put me in these holds, no matter how hard I tried, I couldn't get out of them; I couldn't free myself. I had something bigger and stronger than me holding me down in a position that brought pain, frustration, and weariness.

I can imagine this is how the woman in the Bible must have felt. As much as she probably wanted to get free, for eighteen years, she couldn't. Is that where you are today? Is there an area of your life that makes you feel like you're smothered or as if you can't breathe, move, or even change your position? I know this place is one that often brings the feeling of frustration, and after being frustrated for so long, it can then lead to the feeling of weariness. Don't lose your hope in this place! There is an answer to that stronghold that is on your life!

When my brother put me in those holds, although I did not have the power to free myself, there was someone else in the house who did: my dad! All Daddy had to do was say a simple command and my brother had to remove his grip from me.

What my dad did for me is exactly what Jesus did for the woman. Jesus said to her, "Dear woman, you are healed of your sickness! Then he touched her, and instantly she could stand straight" (verse 12-13 NLT). Jesus got involved in this woman's situation. And whenever He gets involved, things cannot remain the same! He commanded that the enemy loose his grip off of her. Yes, the hold she was in was strong, but Jesus is even stronger! First John 4:4 states, "He who is in you is greater than he who is in the world" (NKJV). There is no hold the enemy can put on you that God will not be able to remove. God is the all-powerful and all-mighty God, and there is none that can compare to Him.

Jesus released and freed this woman of her eighteen-year hold. And what Jesus did for this woman, He wants to do for you! You can be freed TODAY of bondage.

> And whenever He gets involved, things cannot remain the same! There is no hold the enemy can put on you that God will not be able to remove.

The first step requires you to simply believe and have faith that you are no longer held hostage by the enemy. Decree with your mouth, "I am free," believe God to deliver you, and watch His power manifest healing in your life! As you declare that you are free, keep these words spoken by Jesus close to heart:

"So if the Son sets you free, you are truly free" (John 8:36 NLT).

Healing Revelation 5:
I Don't Have to be Afraid Because I've Got God's Presence
Deuteronomy 31:6

Isn't it exciting to watch toddlers walk for the first time? I have watched and witnessed many toddlers learn how to walk. When it is time for them to step into this new chapter of their life, the toddler is assisted by their parent in this new process. The parent holds them by their hand and walks with them as they take their first steps. Notice how unstable the toddler is. Since this is something new for the toddler and because they are wobbly, shaky, and unstable, the parent holds their hands as a guide. Even though the parent will start off holding their hand, at some point, they have to let go. This new chapter is one that requires participation from both the parent and the toddler. The parent has to be willing to let go, and the toddler has to be willing to move on their own. The parent must let go in order for the toddler to gain enough confidence to walk on their own; however, the parent doesn't disappear. They wait patiently, close by the toddler's side, always available just in case their child needs them. The parent allows space for the toddler to grow, but they don't leave the toddler alone. Even though the toddler may not feel the touch of their parent with every step they take, they can be assured that mommy/daddy is right there. The very *presence* of the parent is comforting to the toddler.

The relationship God has with us is very similar to that of a parent to a toddler learning how to walk for the first time. Just like the toddler, we all find ourselves in toddler-like stages of life where we learn to do something for the first time. It could be a new job, a new marriage, a new relationship, a new business, a new location, or even a new degree. Whenever we turn the page in our book of life and arrive at a new chapter, there will usually be some form of uneasiness. This uneasiness is no different than what is experienced by toddlers who've never walked before and are wobbly and shaky when they just start out.

Starting something for the first time will bring a certain level of discomfort and uncertainty. You may even stumble and fall a few times. But it's OK! You are not alone. You see, God is our Heavenly Father, and He is always there by our side with every step that we take. Just like a natural parent when we start something new, God will reach out and hold our hands while we take those first steps. Additionally, just like the natural parent, at some point, God will "let go." Letting go does not mean that God lets go of us literally. But, rather, it means that He will sometimes appear to take a step back just to see how well we will trust His leading even when we may not necessarily feel Him. The way we trust God's leading is simply by leaning and depending on His Word.

In Deuteronomy chapter 31, Moses is preparing the Israelites to cross the Jordan River in order to occupy the land that God promised they shall have. He was also preparing them for a new leader, Joshua. Moses had led these people for many, many years and now they had to turn the page to a new chapter. They had to enter a new land with a new leader. How scary could that have been? I believe Moses could sense the fear that grew amongst the people and that is why he said these words to them in verse 6, "Be strong and of good courage, do not fear nor be afraid of them; for the LORD your God, He *is* the One who goes with you. He will not leave you nor forsake you" (NKJV).

So, what are *you* afraid of? You may be stepping into a new chapter of your life, but you are not stepping into it alone. God is with you! Take the step! Do not be afraid of stumbling or falling; walk anyway! God promised us that He will always be by our side. Yes, there will be times when God may appear to "let go," but He will not leave us. He is only causing our faith and trust in Him to grow stronger. Remember, the parent may have let go of the toddler's hand, but the parent stays by the toddler's side. God is by your side. His very *presence* is a gift to us. We must realize that every morning when we open our eyes to a brand new day, we are encountered with the presence of our God. So, what are you going to do today since you know that you've got the presence of God with you? How will you prove your trust in God's presence in your life? Step out! Walk! Go forth! Start that new thing! You got this!

> You don't have to be afraid, because
> YOU'VE GOT GOD'S PRESENCE!

Healing Revelation 6: I Can Handle Change

Have you ever played the game *Red Light, Green Light*? This was one of the most exciting games I played as a child. The game was simple: if you could follow instructions well, you had a great chance of winning! The leader would stand at a distance from the players and would call out either "red light," "yellow light," or "green light." If the leader said, "green light," the players were to run as fast as they could towards the leader. If the leader said, "yellow light," the players were allowed to keep moving towards the leader; however, they had to do it in a slow fashion. If the leader said, "red light," the players were to remain still. If the player moved in a way that was not granted by the leader, the player would lose their position and had to start from the beginning. For example, if the leader shouted, "red light" and the player moved in any way, they had to start over. In reflecting back on playing that game, I notice that the winner of the game was not necessarily the player who was the quickest but the one who could listen well, i.e., if the player moved too quickly, they would try to "run fast" when the leader really instructed them to "slow down" or "stop." The game *Red Light, Green Light* included a lot of changes, and the players had to have great listening skills in order to manage the changes.

Do you have great listening skills and are you able to manage the changes of your life? We must be able to hear God well in order to adapt to the changes He brings in our lives. There are some seasons where God will command us to move quickly on something. That could mean to quickly make a decision about purchasing insurance due to a tight window of opportunity or to see a certain family member that has been "in our spirit," and unbeknownst to us, may soon pass away. Other times God will command us to move slowly with caution. This may be for a particular relationship to ensure we will steward it well, or it could even be to take our time and study His Word in depth and with meaning. Still, there are times when God commands us to stop and it will be like a big red warning sign. This could be to get our attention because we are heading in the wrong direction. Whether God intends for us to move quickly on some things, slowly, or to stop all together, we must know how God wants us to move and when He is ready for us to change.

Change doesn't always feel good. We don't like to change especially when we've become comfortable with what we have or with where we are, but change is inevitable. It is going to happen whether we want it to or not. So, what are the changes God is commanding you to make in your life? Are you switching jobs or careers? Are you called to full-time ministry? Are you moving from singleness to marriage? Are you shifting from just being a spouse to becoming a parent? Think about the changes God is moving you to make in your life right now or a change you know must come in the near future. How comfortable are you with the change, and how willing is your heart to change *on time*?

Let's take human nature as an example. I live in the state of Virginia and am fortunate to experience all four seasons: Winter, Spring, Summer and Fall. In the Summer, I am very comfortable wearing a short-sleeve shirt and maybe even flip flops with no coat needed. However, if I don't learn to adjust to the temperature changes in the Fall and slowly incorporate long-sleeve shirts and light-weight jackets into my wardrobe, how will I be prepared for the fifty-degree weather in the Winter which will require my coat, scarf, and boots? What would happen if I kept choosing to wear my short-sleeve shirt and flip flops in the snow? Not only would it affect my physical state, but I would also be out of place.

Adapting to the seasons we are in spiritually requires us to listen carefully to what God is saying. He shows us what to do, how to do it, when to do it, and even where to do it. God may tell you to fast for a particular season or to connect with someone specific. He's always speaking and trying to prepare us for what's coming next because He knows what lies ahead. When He speaks, we must know how to respond. Are you responding to His voice?

I know it's difficult to change, but you can handle change! Let this encourage you: you never change on your own, for God is always with you. If you know that you have not been accepting change well and have not responded to God's commands, I invite you now to take a moment and ask Him for forgiveness. Afterwards, I invite you to pray the following prayer with me:

Most Holy God,

I honor who You are in my life, and I thank You for being with me always. Give me the strength and the grace to move as You command. I do not want to miss my moments of opportunities. Help me to be wired to Your every command so that when You speak it, I simply respond without question. I accept my season to change, and I boldly proclaim that I can handle change. In Jesus' name, Amen.

Healing Revelation 7:
God is Perfecting My Faith
Mark 4:35-41

Near the end of Mark chapter 4, Jesus challenges His disciples to get in a boat with Him and cross a lake. If you read the story, you will see that the disciples did in fact get in the boat with Jesus as the evening part of the day was approaching. Soon after they started out on the lake, they found themselves in the midst of a really bad storm. As a result of the storm, the waves became pretty rough and water began to fill the inside of the boat. During this time, Jesus was at the back of the boat sleeping. His disciples began to panic and ran to wake Jesus up. When they woke Him up, they shouted at Him and wondered if He even cared about what was going on. The disciples felt that their lives were threatened and that they were going to die. "When Jesus woke up, he rebuked the wind and said to the waves, 'Silence! Be still!' Suddenly the wind stopped, and there was a great calm. Then he asked them, 'Why are you afraid? Do you still have no faith?'" (Mark 4:39-40 NLT)

Can you picture the disciples on this boat in the middle of a storm? Can you picture strong winds, heavy rain, and the boat being tossed in one direction and then in another? Can you imagine seeing the boat fill with water? Now I want you to picture yourself in a situation that made you feel as though your life was threatened. Was your heart beating fast? Did you panic? Did you cry? Were you overwhelmed with stress and fear? Did you also cry out to God and wondered if He even cared about what you were going through? Maybe you are currently in a great storm right now and it feels like you are literally fighting for your life. What are your thoughts? Is fear stronger than your faith?

Let's dig deeper into this story to see what it was that Jesus was trying to do in His disciples because I believe He is also doing the same thing for you. I truly believe Jesus used this moment to challenge the disciples' faith. Didn't Jesus know that the storm was coming when He asked them to get in the boat? In addition, while in the midst of the storm, Jesus decides to go to sleep. This experience was one that pushed the perfecting of the disciples' faith because Jesus needed *them to see* where *they had put their faith and trust*. Was it in Him or in the boat? Remember, the boat began to fill with water and most of these disciples had been fishermen. Therefore, they had been in plenty of boats and knew how a boat was supposed to operate. They also knew that a boat was not supposed to fill up with water, so when it did, they panicked. It appeared that they put their faith in the boat to get them to where they were going instead of in Jesus. Whenever we put our faith in other things to carry us to where we need to go, God will cause that thing to malfunction so that He can shift where we put our faith and trust.

WHAT IS YOUR BOAT? What have you been depending upon to carry you in this season? What would cause you to panic if it suddenly began to malfunction? Is it your job/career? Is it your bank account? What about your marriage? Or a particular friendship? Could it be your church? When something or someone we trust becomes shaky and unreliable causing us to panic in fear, it is an indication that we are not trusting wholeheartedly in God and that our faith is not in Him alone. God desires for our faith to be only in Him, for He knows everything about us and every detail concerning our situations. So, we must not put our faith in people or things to carry us, but we must know that God is more than capable of safely getting us to where we need to go. Besides, He already knows where we're going anyway.

If you can identify with these disciples and can admit that you have been panicking due to something malfunctioning in your life, it could be God re-shifting where you place your faith and trust. He is the only One that can carry you—let Him. Think it not strange that a relationship is ending or your job let you go. Trust that God is only moving some things around so that your faith is in Him and Him alone.

So what if the boat is filling with water? Do what Jesus did—relax and go to sleep! Let God take over from here and let Him perfect your faith.

> Whenever we put our faith in other things to carry us to where we need to go, God will cause that thing to malfunction so that He can shift where we put our faith and trust.

I encourage you to utilize the lines below to demand your separation from some people, places, or things that you have been relying on to carry you.

My faith is no longer in _____

_____ to carry me!

My faith is no longer in _____

_____ to carry me!

My faith is no longer in _____

_____ to carry me!

My faith is no longer in _____

_____ to carry me!

My faith is no longer in _____

_____ to carry me!

Healing Revelation 8:
I Have a New Mind
1 Peter 5:8-9

About eight years ago I decided to try and have fish as pets. I was so excited. I bought four small Guppies. I then bought a one-gallon purple fish tank to put them in, and I even had rocks, pebbles, and greenery to put in the tank as decorations. Prior to purchasing the fish, I did research. I learned the best ways to acclimate fish to new environments. The day came when I brought the fish home. I put them in their tank and watched them as they explored their new home. The next day, I went to work as usual, came home, and saw my wonderful fish. I watched them as they swam around in the tank. On the following day, I went to work as usual, came home, and, again, watched my fish swim around in the tank. I was getting used to this. When the next day came, I went to work as usual, came home, but all four of my fish had died. I was sad, disappointed, and confused. I talked to a professional and inquired about what could have gone wrong. They told me that because the fish tank was so small, it most likely overwhelmed the fish. The tank wasn't big enough to handle the fish. They felt confined and cluttered, so they died.

This is exactly what the enemy wants to do to your mind, i.e., to place your mind in a state of confinement. He wants you to feel as though you are in a prison. He does this by clouding your mind with negative thoughts. He wants you to be so consumed by negative thinking that you eventually become overwhelmed. And when you get to the place where you are overwhelmed, you start to shut down and everything in you begins to die. You die on the inside when you lose focus of your assignments simply because you're too concerned about your thoughts. You die on the inside when you cry more and laugh less all because you're too caught up on the "should haves," "would haves," and "could haves." The enemy wants you to be so overwhelmed in your mind that you begin to die and cannot function.

One of the tactics that the enemy used in my life caused me to overanalyze everything that I said. It was hard to have conversations with people without me wondering if I said something wrong. It got so bad that I would lose focus on what I was supposed to be doing that day because I was so concerned that I said something offensive to someone else. God really helped me and continues to help me in this area. He started challenging me to "once and for all" replay in my head what it was that I said. Many times, after replaying it, I realized that I sounded dumb just thinking about it. God helped me to learn how to quickly let go of being overly concerned about what I say and even do. Even today the thoughts may still come, but I don't spend all day wondering, *Did I offend her when I said that?* Now, I just simply replay the situation in my mind and whether what I said was wrong or not, I ask God to forgive me so that I can let it go and move on.

Do you have negative thoughts clouding your mind on a consistent basis? Do you worry and wonder about what people are thinking about you? Do you overanalyze every word that comes out of your mouth? Are you so preoccupied with past situations that you can't change? Can I encourage you today, my brother, my sister? Let those thoughts go. Do not allow the enemy to have a field day in your mind. Make the choice that every time a negative thought comes into your mind, you will choose to think positive on purpose. I know this sounds elementary, but it works! Tell that devil, "Nope, you can't get me with that!" Your thoughts are powerful because they turn into your actions. Your actions should be centered around what God assigned you to do and not paranoia as a result of negative thinking.

First Peter 5:8-9 declares, "Stay alert! Watch out for your great enemy, the devil. He prowls around like a roaring lion, looking for someone to devour. Stand firm against him, and be strong in your faith..." (NLT) This clearly encourages us to always be on our guard and recognize that the enemy is always plotting and planning against us. It is the battle over your mind that he wants, but he can only win if you let him. YOU can HAVE A

NEW MIND if you work for it. So, today, let us take a stand together and decree and declare that I Have A New Mind!

This next assignment is in two parts:

1. Ask God to help you know how the enemy attacks *your* mind. You want to be clear in recognizing his strategies.

_____

_____

_____

_____

_____

2. Ask God to help you figure out what it will take for you to be free in your mind. This will be different for each person as God created us to be unique individuals.

_____

_____

_____

_____

_____

Healing Revelation 9:
I Am Pregnant with God's Promises
Luke 1:26-38

In Luke chapter 1, little did Mary know that she would become pregnant with God's promise! The angel Gabriel visited Mary to inform her that she had found favor with God and would conceive a son whom she was to name 'Jesus.' I'd like to bring attention to verse 34 for Mary was unsure of how she could possibly conceive. She inquired, "But how can this happen? I am a virgin" (NLT). Mary, thinking with her human mind, could not understand how it would be possible to conceive without her having to get physically involved. Because of her condition (being a virgin), she thought it was impossible for her to conceive a child.

Has God spoken some things over you and told you that you would become something more than you are? Or that you would have the ability to accomplish some things that you never even thought about? How did you feel when God spoke that to you? Like Mary, were you surprised and with a raised eyebrow, thought, *But how can this happen?* Mary was in a condition that to humans would make conception impossible. What condition are you in that is making you feel that it is impossible for you to conceive and give birth to the promises of God in your life?

Let me send some encouragement your way. You do not have to feel that you can't possibly be used by God because of your past addictions, sins, missed opportunities, hiccups, or failed attempts. Do not think any less of yourself because of your hurts, pains, and heartbreaks. Don't allow the enemy to make you feel that because you do not have the degree you cannot do what God has asked of you. Stop listening to lies that you are not special—you are not a mistake! And God did not make a mistake when He caused your spiritual womb to conceive His promises for your life!

You, yes YOU, are PREGNANT WITH GOD'S PROMISES! How, you ask? This is the Holy Spirit's doing. You may even be questioning what you are pregnant with. God has specific gifts, abilities, calling(s), and assignments that He only assigned to you. What you are carrying are the things that God is going to use you to do for His glory. What has God been speaking and revealing to you? You have unique gifts in you and what God gave to you is just for you! Embrace this pregnancy! The baby inside of you is Holy!

All that you have to do is accept the fact that God chose you to carry something, and when the time is right (God's timing), you will give birth to the promises of God in your life!

It's time to put your faith into action! Using the lines below, create a list of what you already know God has promised would manifest in your life:

_____

_____

_____

_____

_____

Maybe you have already given birth to some things. If so, write them out on the lines below to remind you of what God has already done for you!

_____

_____

_____

_____

_____

Healing Revelation 10:
I Am Not Who I Used to Be
John 9:1-11

The word *reputation* is defined as an "overall quality or character as seen or judged by people in general." What is your current reputation? What do people think about you or even know about you? What would you like your reputation to be in the future? How do you want people to remember you when you are no longer here on earth? Now, what is your past reputation? Many times, people will hold us to the person that we once were. You could be ten years free from smoking, but someone who knew you as a smoker may still see you as one. Why is it so hard for society to accept the fact that people really do change?

I'd like to point out a man who is discussed in John chapter 9. This man is said to have been blind from birth. As Jesus approached the man, He spat on the ground, made mud, and placed the mud over the blind man's eyes. Then Jesus told the man to go to the pool of Siloam to wash. The man did as Jesus said, and after he washed, he was able to see! (John 9:1,6-7) Take note of the people in his community. "His neighbors and others *who knew him as a blind beggar* asked each other, 'Isn't this the man who used to sit and beg?' Some said he was, and others said, '*No, he just looks like him!*'" (John 9:8-9 NLT) Some of the man's neighbors knew who he was in his past and refused to believe that the man who could now see was the same man who was once blind. Why was it so hard for them to believe that he was the same man, you may ask? Perhaps it was because they did not believe that a miracle such as this one could really happen. They may have believed that the condition he was in was too difficult for him to come out.

You just might have some people in your life who knew who you used to be in your past and just can't seem to accept the fact that you are a changed person today. Hmm . . . is the person in disbelief **you**? The Bible declares that if you belong to Christ Jesus then YOU are a new person! (2 Corinthians 5:17) You can't stay the exact same when you accept Jesus in your heart to be your Lord and Savior. The moment you accept Him, Jesus begins working on you, in you, and through you to remove what's unlike Him and replace it with His likeness. Believe it or not, YOU ARE A CHANGED PERSON!

Even if you desire to be free from addictions, bad habits, and even some relationships, you can speak these words into the atmosphere right now: "I AM NOT WHO I USED TO BE" and freedom shall be yours! As a matter of fact, the more you say it and the more you believe it, the more you will grow away from those things because God will begin to change your appetite so that you won't even desire to do some of the things you used to do. The amazing thing about this is you may not even see it while it's happening; but one day, you will notice that you have changed. For example, perhaps you were used to smoking a pack of cigarettes a day and begin to wholeheartedly believe God for your breakthrough. By stating this simple affirmation aloud each day (along with other specific affirmations explained below), you may find that hours have gone by before you realize you haven't even smoked one cigarette yet.

> You can't stay the exact same when you accept Jesus in your heart to be your Lord and Savior. The moment you accept Him, Jesus begins working on you, in you, and through you . . .

Or perhaps you desire to be free from a particular relationship because you don't like the person you have become because of it. Again, if you believe God that you are a changed person and declare your affirmation(s) aloud, two, three, or even four days will past before you realize you haven't even desired to talk to them on the phone! Yes, change really CAN happen, and if you believe you are a changed person, it CAN HAPPEN TO YOU! Isn't the love of God so incredible?

So, here's the million-dollar question: from what are you believing God that you are changed? I invite you, right now, to SPEAK ALOUD the things from which you are believing God to deliver you.

After doing so, speak this simple affirmation aloud: I Am Not Who I Used To Be!

But don't stop there! I now challenge you to create your own affirmations below about this new change, and be SPECIFIC! I believe that *true change comes when you can be honest and admit what you need to be changed.* I've included an example for you.

Example: _____ I No Longer Desire to Smoke Cigarettes _____

_____

_____

_____

_____

Remember, brothers and sisters, the more you say it and the more you believe it, the further you are away from it . . . watch God change your appetite!

Healing Revelation 11:
I Have What It Takes to Win

Before bakers bake a cake, they have to decide exactly which ingredients they want to put into their cake, e.g., what kind of cake to make, how many eggs to use, which type of oil, what brand of butter, how much flour, etc. Making a cake requires a detailed thought process. Once they are ready, they combine all of the ingredients together, mix them well, pour the cake mixture into a baking dish, and finally place the baking dish in the oven. The cake then has to stay in the oven long enough for all of the ingredients to take their rightful place in the cake. When the ingredients are all in their rightful place, the cake is ready to come out.

What's interesting about a cake is that it does not matter whether you decide to take a piece from the left side or the right, or whether you go straight to the middle of the cake, because all of the pieces will taste the exact same. The reason why they taste the exact same is because they all have the exact same ingredients. Any part of the cake will give you the same results. I'd like to think about God creating us in this same way. When He created us, He put everything in us that would give us the potential to become who He designed for us to be.

If you feel as though your life is pointless and that God is not concerned about you, I'd like to speak directly to you. God has great plans for you, and His plans about your life were already in His mind long before you even touched this earth. The enemy, the devil, lied to you when he told you that you were not meant to live, for everything that God created He saw that it was good (Genesis 1). My purpose here is to help you see your purpose for living and then to give you the tools needed to strive to live!

God has something specific for you to do while here on

earth, and when He created you, He put in you what you would need to accomplish everything He set out for you. God also created us to be able to handle any obstacle, issue, or problem that we would face in life. It is Satan's desire to keep you from becoming who God created you to be. Therefore, he will use whatever he wants to throw off your focus from your destiny. The enemy is after the anointing on your life, your sanity, and ultimately, your faith and trust in God. He wants to try and break up your relationship with God. He knows that he cannot get God to turn His back on you, so he tries to get you to turn your back on God. How, you ask? He does this by sending attacks in your life by trying to cause illnesses, confusion in the household, division in the family, issues on the job, drama in the church, and so on. Be aware of the devil's attacks in your life!

> God has great plans for you, and His plans about your life were already in His mind long before you even touched this earth.

But wait, friend . . . YOU ALREADY HAVE WHAT IT TAKES TO WIN AGAINST EVERY ATTACK THE ENEMY THROWS AT YOUR LIFE! Just like the cake will give you the same results no matter which part of it you take from, so should we have the same level of faith no matter which area of our lives the enemy tries to attack!

With every attack the enemy sends your way, fight him with the Word of God! So even if the devil tries to attack your finances, health, marriage, children, business, ministry, or even your mind, know that God has already made you to be a WINNER! Here are some tips to help you WIN in every situation against the enemy:

- Maintain constant communication and devotion with God.

- Create a place in your own home and worship God!

- Open your Bible and remind yourself of the promises of God in your life.

- Fast and pray and trust God to lead you.

- Use your mouth to declare that you are a child of the Most High God and that you've already won!

My brother, my sister, you've got this! It doesn't matter what area of your life the enemy tries to attack because God created you to WIN!

Healing Revelation 12:
I Yield to God's Voice
Luke 5:1-6

Imagine something with me. Let's say that you are a fisherman and you take your boat out to catch some fish. Here you are, out on the boat with your fishing line in the water expecting to catch fish. Occasionally, you draw in your line to replace the bait and toss it back out in the water. It's hot, muggy, and you're tired and sweaty. You go all evening and all night and end up catching nothing. So, you head back to shore with nothing. Then the next day, a man comes by and tells you to take your boat back out into the water and throw your fishing line into the water again. How would you feel? Would you do it?

I have just outlined for you what actually happened to Simon, later known as Peter, in the beginning of Luke chapter 5. He had been out fishing all night and was unable to catch anything. Jesus comes along the next day, teaches the crowd from Simon's boat, and after teaching, tells Simon to take his boat out into deep water and to throw out his nets there. Initially, Simon explains to Jesus that he had already been out the entire previous night which had been very unsuccessful. However, regardless of how tired and frustrated he probably was, he says to Jesus, "...But if you say so, I'll let the nets down again" (verse 5 NLT).

My brother and sister, you may be in a season where you have to *hear your way out* of it. Our deliverance, breakthrough, and healing are connected to our obedience to God's instructions. What is God instructing you to do right now in your life? It could be that your obedience and willingness to yield to His voice are the very things that will shift you into the right position to receive the blessings of God in your life.

When we choose not to listen to God and do what He asks of us, we don't know what blessings we are hindering ourselves from receiving. What if Simon refused to listen to Jesus? If he depended on his yesterday's experience of a failed attempt and disobeyed Jesus, he would have missed out on the BIGGEST catch he's probably ever had!

Simon chose to obey Jesus by having an "if you say so" mentality. Sometimes, that's all the understanding we need, i.e., "Because God said so." We must stop trying to figure out step B, C, and D, and just simply complete step A all because "God said so." If you will make up in your mind to yield to God's voice right where you are, no matter what failures you have had in the past, I truly believe you will see the hand of the Lord deliver GREAT blessings your way!

In fact, Simon caught so much fish that his net began to tear! He had to ask for help from some of his partners and both of their boats ended up being filled with fish! Are you ready to receive a blessing so great that you will need help receiving it all?! Then you must YIELD TO GOD'S VOICE! Do what it is that God is telling you to do! Your obedience to God's voice is not just for you but those connected to you will also be affected! Make the decision this moment to go back in your mind, look back at your journal, and remind yourself of the instructions God has given to you, and watch the healing, deliverance, and breakthrough that come as a result of your obedience! Yield to God's Voice!

What has God instructed you to do?

1. _____

_____

2. _____

_____

3. _____

_____

4. _____

_____

5. _____

_____

Healing Revelation 13:
I Have a Purpose for Living
Jeremiah 1:4-5

I am a fan of the American sport, football. I look forward to the time of year when Summer meets Fall because that is when the new football season begins. It is exciting and intriguing to see the various talents on the football field. For many players, especially those who reach the level of professional football, they, along with their parents, notice a distinct quality about themselves early on in life. They may have the ability to run faster than their peers or just simply have an interest in playing football at a young age. For these select persons–athletes–their life purpose (or one of their life's purposes) has been detected early. Evidence of this purpose is proven when they are on the field engaging in their gifts, talents, and skills.

Well, football players and other athletes are not the only ones who have a purpose for living life—we all do. God put purpose in all of us; it is up to us to seek God for clarity on that purpose and then to accept it, believe in it, and trust God to help us with walking it out. Just in case you are reading this message and you thought that you did not have a reason for being alive, today is your "blessed" day! I am excited to tell you that YOU, yes YOU, have a purpose for living!

Look at these verses from the prophet Jeremiah, "The LORD gave me this message: 'I knew you before I formed you in your mother's womb. Before you were born I set you apart and appointed you as my prophet to the nations'" (Jeremiah 1:4-5 NLT). The Lord God informed Jeremiah that even before he entered this world, God had already put a purpose inside of him and that purpose would bring glory and honor to God. God has done this exact same thing with all of His creation. I don't believe

God makes something without purpose because even if you read the creation account in Genesis chapter 1, you will see that with everything God created, He also had a purpose for its existence.

Before you first stepped into this world, God had already put a purpose inside of you. Therefore, on the day you were born, you were not born empty, but you were born with purpose. Let's look at Jesus. Ultimately, Jesus was sent to earth to die on the cross for our sins so that we all might have life eternal. Well, did Jesus come out of the womb as a full-grown adult? Of course not! Furthermore, even as a baby, He was still holy, and His purpose was already there. He was still the Savior even from birth (Luke 1:31-35; Luke 2:11-12). Let this encourage you, friend, that on the day you were born, no matter how you got here, you were already filled with purpose from God!

Maybe, you have felt so unworthy to live that you've question why you are even here. Or, maybe you've even tried to take your own life. It is a trick of Satan to make you feel as though your birth was a mistake. It does not matter if your birth was one that was planned, unplanned, or even as a result of sinful nature, God shaped and formed you in your mother's womb because He had a special purpose for your existence!

What is your purpose for living? Only God can answer that question for you. What I can tell you, however, is that whatever your purpose is, it has been designed to give glory and honor to God. In order to find out what God has put on the inside of you, all you have to do is _ask_ Him.

I'd like to share with you a personal story:

I am a licensed minister of the Gospel and have been given the gift and ability to preach and teach. I was seventeen years old when I first heard the call to preach. Someone had called me out in a church service and said, "Brittney, you will preach a Word one day." I wasn't sure how to receive that, and by being so young, I pushed it to the back of my mind. After the first time I heard the call, two months later, God used a different person to speak on my call to preach the Gospel. At that time, I began to think about it more often. I even stepped out towards my purpose, however, I became afraid and ceased my pursuit of it. A year and a half went by and I wasn't moving towards my purpose, and needless to say, it wasn't leaving me alone either. It felt as though it was attached to me. It was on my mind frequently and I just could not escape it. At the end of that year and a half, I finally asked God that if He really wanted me to preach to tell me again. Two to three months after I *asked* God about my purpose, He answered. A minister at the church I was attending came to me after morning worship service. He introduced himself and said to me, "I don't know who you are, but I know you are a preacher." Immediately, I started to laugh. That day God told me, "Never again second guess your calling." From that day on, I accepted it, believed in it, and trusted God to help me to walk it out. I must say, that was the best decision I have made.

I hope my personal story has been helpful to you. It is not my assignment to tell you what your purpose is, but I am to encourage you to know that YOU HAVE A PURPOSE FOR LIVING! Let today be the first day that you take a step towards your purpose even if that simply means that you ask God to show you your purpose. If you already know your purpose, then I simply want to cheer you on as you continue to boldly live out your purpose!

Here's an opportunity for you to visually see your purpose: write it out! What is your purpose? (Even if you don't know now, wait until God shows you and then write it/them on the lines below.)

_____

_____

_____

_____

Healing Revelation 14:
I Am Not Bound by the Wound
Part 1: The Initial Cut

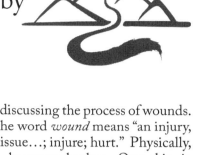

I'd like to spend time with you discussing the process of wounds. According to the dictionary, the word *wound* means "an injury, usually involving division of tissue…; injure; hurt." Physically, a wound occurs when the skin becomes broken. Our skin is broken when something sharp pierces the body which causes an *interruption* in the body's normal functioning. When this happens, the body becomes wounded. Wounds are not comfortable because they bring pain. Whether it is a small papercut or a deep tissue puncture, wounds cause pain. Not only do they cause pain but the majority of the time they can lead to bleeding. When the body bleeds, physically it is a sign that something has gotten in too close. Skin was designed to serve as a layer of protection for the body; however, when its purpose has been compromised, it is a threat to the body's security system. **WOUNDS** . . . they leave the body in a state of brokenness.

Let's now look at the word *wound* in an intangible way. Sometimes life can cause us to experience mental or emotional wounds. Just like the physical wound, emotional/mental wounds occur when situations happen that cause an *interruption* in our normal daily functioning. Maybe you've just lost a loved one. Maybe your job unexpectedly ended. Maybe your marriage is experiencing a rocky season or the child you've loved and nurtured has now turned their back on you. Or maybe ministry isn't quite working out the way that you thought it would or the same people you worship with on Sunday morning are talking about you behind your back Monday through Saturday. **WOUNDS**. A wound occurs when something that you have depended on as a layer of protection becomes broken and it is a threat to your security system. You are wounded when you feel as though your heart is bleeding, and with every breath, you breathe in pain and breathe out misery.

Have you been wounded? Are you currently wounded right now? You may have even asked the questions, "WHEN IS IT OVER? When does the pain stop?" There is never an easy answer to pain. But, can I encourage you today with these words? "So humble yourselves under the mighty power of God, and at the right time he will lift you up in honor. Give all your worries and cares to God, for he cares about you ... So after you have suffered a little while, he will restore, support, and strengthen you, and he will place you on a firm foundation" (1 Peter 5:6-7,10 NLT).

Here in the book of 1 Peter chapter 5, it states that whatever your *care* is—meaning your struggle, concern, heartache, or anything that has caused an *interruption* in your life—you can take it to God. That thing that has pierced your heart—God wants it. That person that has taken away your ability to trust people—God wants it. That situation that left you broken—yes, God wants that, too. Take every hurt, pain, and wound to God. Wounds do not have to control you. When something has <u>bound</u> you, it has control over you. The enemy will lie to you and make you believe that, because you have been wounded, whatever has wounded you has control over you. But he is a liar! Allow God the opportunity to heal your wounds. He is an expert in healing wounds. Why don't you give Him yours today? There is so much more to life, and you have so much more to live for. Regardless of how bad the wound is, the sun does shine again, the wind will stop blowing, and the night will soon turn into the day.

You may have been wounded, but you are not bound by it—it does not have control over you!

Your healing revelation for today is to do something that you would not normally do because of the wound:

-Be happy on purpose

-Speak to someone that doesn't like speaking to you

-Pray and give God the thing that bothers you the most

These are just examples, but you can do all these and more. Why? Because YOU ARE NOT BOUND BY THE WOUND.

I encourage you to list your wounds, past and present, on the lines below (wounds can be people, places, or things) and watch God heal.

I Am Not Bound By _____

_____

I Am Not Bound By _____

_____

I Am Not Bound By _____

_____

I Am Not Bound By _____

_____

I Am Not Bound By _____

_____

Remember, the more you say it, the more you will believe it. I Am Not Bound By The Wound!

Healing Revelation 15:
I Am Not Bound by the Wound
Part 2: The Cleansing

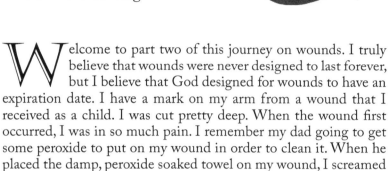

Welcome to part two of this journey on wounds. I truly believe that wounds were never designed to last forever, but I believe that God designed for wounds to have an expiration date. I have a mark on my arm from a wound that I received as a child. I was cut pretty deep. When the wound first occurred, I was in so much pain. I remember my dad going to get some peroxide to put on my wound in order to clean it. When he placed the damp, peroxide soaked towel on my wound, I screamed like there was no tomorrow! That hurt worse than the wound itself! Although he knew that the peroxide would cause more pain, he applied it to my wound anyway, because *daddy knew* that peroxide *was necessary* in order to keep the wound from becoming infected.

Are you in a cleansing stage of your wound? While reading this message right now, perhaps you have already been wounded. And maybe you have even given your situation to God. Yet, you still feel pain. May I suggest to you that maybe this particular pain you feel is not the wound itself but the hand of God cleansing your wound so that you will not become infected?

How does God cleanse a wound? God can do this in so many various ways. One example could be by putting a restraint on your connections with certain people, places, or things. Has God forbidden you from engaging in a certain relationship? Has God told you to leave a job which was your only means of income (so you thought)? Or has God given you specific instructions to stay away from a particular location? When God puts certain restraints on us, though the restraints bring a certain level of pain, they are necessary for our spiritual, physical, emotional, and mental health. If God purposefully instructs you to stay away from someone or something, it could be because being connected to them or it would spread toxins in your life and infections would occur. Another example could be God positioning you in a place that is very uncomfortable. This could be going back to school, starting a new business or ministry, or even joining a new church. Being placed in uncomfortable positions are also necessary for our health because if God allowed us to stay in the same places our entire life—places that are no longer helping us but hurting us— we might become infected. But, because we are so comfortable, we would never know it.

> Do not allow the evil one to deceive you into thinking that you do not need to listen to the voice of God. Do whatever God tells you to do.

Every directive that God gives us is for a greater purpose and plan. Though God may have asked you to do something(s) that has brought you pain, He knows *it is necessary* to keep you from becoming infected.

Be careful! Do not allow the evil one to deceive you into thinking that you do not need to listen to the voice of God. Do whatever God tells you to do. Your obedience to the voice of God may bring some pain, but it is necessary for your health. This pain may just be God's way of cleansing you so that you don't become infected with toxins.

You can do this! Go wherever God tells you to go, say whatever God tells you to say, and do whatever God tells you to do. In this way, you are proving to yourself and the enemy that YOU ARE NOT BOUND BY THE WOUND!

I encourage you to pray the following prayer and trust God for clarity:

Most Holy God,

I acknowledge your Sovereignty. I ask that You make clear to me the areas in my life where You are cleansing me. Show me who or what I need to disconnect from so that I will not become infected with the things that are not of You. You promised that Your grace is sufficient. Please give me the grace to endure the cleansing processes of life. Teach me Your Will for my life. And Father, I thank You that I Am Not Bound by the Wound.

In Jesus' name, Amen.

Healing Revelation 16:
I Am Not Bound by the Wound
Part 3: The Scar

Congratulations, you've made it to part three on wounds, and I would like to invite you to explore with me *the scar*. As I have mentioned in part two, wounds were never meant to last forever but they do have an expiration date. When a wound expires, it becomes a scar. A *scar* is defined as "a mark left by a healed wound, sore, or burn." A scar is a wound that was *healed*. I also mentioned to you about the "mark" on my arm from a wound I received as a child. That mark is actually a scar. Recently I looked at the scar on my arm and God gave me a new revelation. He said, "Brittney, when you look at that scar, you can think about one or two things: you can either think about all the pain you went through **OR** you can think about the fact that it was Me who took the pain away."

Do you have scars?

During a conversation I had with my mother about wounds and scars, she reminded me of our Savior, Jesus, who also had to go through the process of being wounded. When the time came for Jesus to be crucified on the cross, they stuck a crown made of thorns on His head and struck Him on the head with a stick (Matthew 27:29-30). Because of this, the thorns most likely pierced His head and He became wounded. At the site of His crucifixion, Jesus was nailed to a cross with a nail driven in each one of His hands and in His feet (Psalms 22:16; Matthew 27:35). Each nail broke into His body and He became wounded. After going through the pains of being wounded on the cross, Jesus died on that cross—the place of His wounds. His body was even laid in a tomb and the last that people knew at that time was a wounded Jesus. Jesus knows what it's like to be wounded. He knows what it's like to be in pain. But He also knows that wounds don't last forever, for even His wounds had an expiration date.

In John chapter 20, after Jesus resurrected from the dead, He appeared to His disciples who were together in a locked room (verse 19). This was the first time His disciples saw Him alive. The last time they saw Him, He had died on the cross and His body was laid in a tomb. But Jesus appeared to them and He specifically showed them His wounds (verse 20). He showed them His wounds so that they would know that He was the same One that had died but has now been raised to life again. He was proving to them that His wounds did not defeat Him.

Yes, Jesus had to deal with wounds. When His enemies nailed Him to the cross, He was wounded. When they put His body in the grave, He was wounded. Jesus reappeared to His disciples after the Spirit of God resurrected Him from the grave to prove to them that He was in fact the Savior who was NOT BOUND BY THE WOUNDS. Yes, Jesus had been wounded, but He lets us know that He was not bound by them.

So, dear friends, where are you scarred in your life? When you look back at your scar(s), do they bring you pain? With every scar(s) that you have in your life, may I encourage you that when you now look at your scar(s), do not think about all the pain that the wound cost you. Don't think about the misery you had to endure. Don't think about all the sleepless nights you spent pacing the floor. Don't think about your failures, hiccups, slip-ups, or screw ups. But now, when you look at that scar, be reminded that it was God who healed you. It was God who took the pain away. It was God who wiped every tear you cried. It was God who cared for you. It was God who protected you, provided for you, and kept you. It was God who gave you another chance. It was God who took your mess and gave you a new beginning. God made sure that you would not be bound by the wound! Thank and praise God for His faithfulness in your life!

The scar is just a reminder to us that God has healed us from our wound. I knew I was completely healed of my wound on my arm when I could run my fingers across it and it no longer registered any pain. You will know that you are truly healed from your wound when you can go back to that place of pain and feel pain no more. Why not believe God today for your complete healing? One more time, say it with me: **I Am Not Bound By The Wound.**

Today's exercise will require faith. I want you to think about the scars in your life and see yourself no longer feeling pain from your memories of being wounded. You can do this!

I am believing by faith that these scars in my life no longer bring me pain:

_____

_____

_____

_____

_____

P.S. Every scar in your life means that you have a testimony! Go tell someone about the wounds that God has healed you from and how you are no longer bound by them!

Healing Revelation 17:

(I invite you to write out your own Healing Revelation)

Why did you choose this revelation and in what ways will it help to manifest healing in your life?

_____

_____

_____

_____

_____

_____

_____

_____

_____

About the Author

Brittney J. Lyons is passionate about serving God and caring for His people. She is a Christian, wife, preacher, teacher, and an inspiring game changer for Christ Jesus. She currently resides in the state of Virginia with her husband, Joseph. She received her Master of Divinity degree from Regent University, Virginia Beach, Virginia. She is the owner and founder of Charis Ministries, a healing ministry. It is her desire to fulfill every divine assignment that God has placed on her path and she is willing to serve God's people through preaching and teaching the Gospel, prayer, or even by a word of encouragement. With the aid of the Holy Spirit, this woman of God will seek to provide the people of God with helpful tools they can use to begin to walk through their journey of HEALING.